WOMEN IN STEM

WOMEN IN ENGINEERING

by Tammy Gagne

Content Consultant
Amy Bix
Professor of History
Iowa State University

Core Library

An Imprint of Abdo Publishing
abdopublishing.com

abdopublishing.com

Published by Abdo Publishing, a division of ABDO, PO Box 398166, Minneapolis, Minnesota 55439. Copyright © 2017 by Abdo Consulting Group, Inc. International copyrights reserved in all countries. No part of this book may be reproduced in any form without written permission from the publisher. Core Library™ is a trademark and logo of Abdo Publishing.

Printed in the United States of America, North Mankato, Minnesota
032016
092016

Cover Photo: Monty Rakusen/Corbis
Interior Photos: Ernest R. Prim/Shutterstock Images, 4; Red Line Editorial, 7, 40; NASA, 9; Everett Historical/Shutterstock Images, 12; Bettmann/Corbis, 15, 43; Shutterstock Images, 20; Xaume Olleros/Bloomberg/Getty Images, 23, 45; Eric Risberg/AP Images, 26; Market Wire/AP Images, 31; Richard Drew/AP Images, 32; Benjamin Beytekin/picture-alliance/dpa/AP Images, 29; Derik Holtmann/Belleville News-Democrat/MCT/Getty Images, 34; Brandon Dill/The Commercial Appeal/AP Images, 37

Editor: Arnold Ringstad
Series Designer: Laura Polzin

Cataloging-in-Publication Data
Names: Gagne, Tammy, author.
Title: Women in engineering / by Tammy Gagne.
Description: Minneapolis, MN : Abdo Publishing, [2017] | Series: Women in
    STEM | Includes bibliographical references and index.
Identifiers: LCCN 2015960518 | ISBN 9781680782677 (lib. bdg.) |
    ISBN 9781680776782 (ebook)
Subjects: LCSH: Women in engineering--Juvenile literature. | Women engineers--
    Juvenile literature.
Classification: DDC 620--dc23
LC record available at http://lccn.loc.gov/2015960518

CONTENTS

CHAPTER ONE
Building the World 4

CHAPTER TWO
Forging the Path 12

CHAPTER THREE
Making a Difference 20

CHAPTER FOUR
**Moving Up and
Advancing Technology** 26

CHAPTER FIVE
Engineering the Future 34

Getting Involved 42

Stop and Think 44

Glossary 46

Learn More 47

Index 48

About the Author 48

BUILDING THE WORLD

Think about a simple trip to school. A student puts on her backpack. An engineer designed it to be strong and sturdy. The student waits at the bus stop. She watches the bus drive down the smooth road. An engineer designed this road too. The bus itself was carefully engineered. It provides a safe ride. The student texts her friends. Engineers designed

Many kinds of engineering are at work behind a simple ride on a school bus.

each part of her smartphone. The work of engineers is all around us.

Engineers use science and creative thinking to design objects and processes that solve practical problems. Some engineering feats save lives. These include safe cars and buildings. Others make life more fun. These include devices that play movies and music. Many engineers build technology that helps the environment. Solar panels and wind turbines, for example, create electricity without polluting. In all areas of engineering, women are making a difference.

Engineers must earn college degrees in their chosen fields. They need to know more than math and science. Engineers must be able to communicate their ideas. They should be good at working with teams. And they should understand the social responsibility behind their work.

Today's engineers work in many settings. Some work for the government. They may help build rockets at NASA. Others work at large companies. They

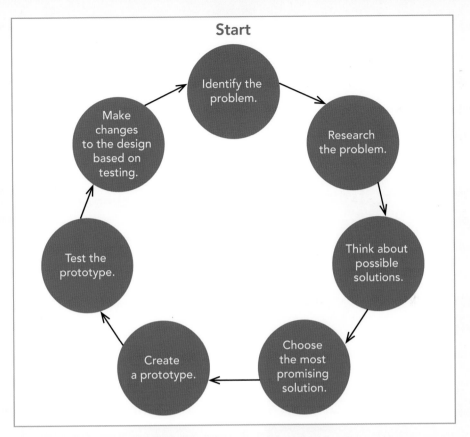

Start

Identify the problem.

Research the problem.

Think about possible solutions.

Choose the most promising solution.

Create a prototype.

Test the prototype.

Make changes to the design based on testing.

The Engineering Design Process

Nearly all engineers follow a process they call the engineering design process. This multistep plan helps them identify needs, create solutions, and improve their designs. Take a look at the steps above. What might happen if an engineer skipped one of these steps?

may design computers at Apple or cars at General Motors. Some work in small start-up companies. They may create the latest popular website. Finally, some engineers are teachers. They teach high school and college students about their field.

A Growing Number

Women have played a major role in the history of engineering. However, the number of female engineers today is relatively low. In 2014 only 11 percent of US engineers were women.

This number is likely to rise in the future. Many young women are studying engineering. Twenty percent of US engineering students in 2015 were female. Some schools saw even higher figures. The University of Pennsylvania reported

Engineer Mary Lobo tests spacecraft parts in large, airless chambers to make sure they work in extreme conditions.

in 2015 that 37 percent of its incoming engineering class was female. Many engineers and educators are committed to increasing gender diversity.

Why Engineering Rocks

Advanced technology is important to daily life. We rely on computers to keep in touch with friends, do work, and have fun. Many engineers are needed to develop these exciting new technologies. At the same time, engineers must maintain and improve our basic infrastructure. This includes objects and structures such as roads, bridges, and power lines. They need civil engineers to keep them working safely.

In 2015 the US government projected 53,700 new job openings for civil engineers by 2022. Other types of engineers will be in high demand too. This demand means engineers can earn high salaries. Many earn more than $100,000 per year. This is far above the national average.

Women in Engineering

The Institute of Electrical and Electronics Engineers has created an organization called Women in Engineering (WIE). It encourages women to pursue careers in this field. WIE gives awards for outstanding achievements by female engineers. In 2013 Ruzena Bajcsy won an award for her work in robotics. WIE also works to inspire young girls. Its mentoring program introduces female students to women who are working in the field.

The field of engineering is broad. It offers a large selection of careers. Many women are drawn to these fields because they offer a chance to improve society. Engineers can use their creativity to make the world a better place.

FURTHER EVIDENCE

Chapter One discusses female engineers and the kinds of work they do. What is one of the main ideas of this chapter? The article below discusses efforts to make engineering more diverse. Find a quote from the article that supports an idea from this chapter. What new information did you learn from this article?

#iLookLikeAnEngineer

mycorelibrary.com/women-in-engineering

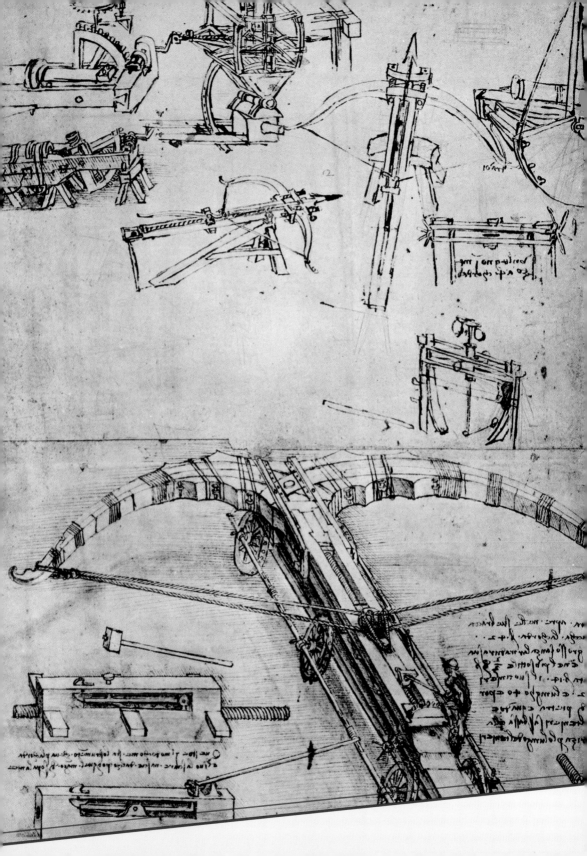

CHAPTER TWO

FORGING THE PATH

The word *engineering* comes from Latin. It means "to devise or think up." People have been inventing tools to make life better for thousands of years. One of the first modern engineers was Leonardo da Vinci. He worked in the late 1400s and early 1500s. Da Vinci and other engineers helped create military weapons. They also made practical products.

In his notebooks, Leonardo da Vinci drew up plans for many inventions.

By the 1800s, engineers had made cities larger. They made farms more productive. Electricity made many new inventions possible. The earliest engineers had not needed formal education. They simply learned as they worked. But the field of human knowledge grew greatly in the 1800s. Engineers needed to know more complex math, physics, and chemistry.

The first female engineers changed the world by pursuing careers in the field. They opened doors for other women. At the same time, they made their own contributions to the history of engineering.

Edith Clarke

Edith Clarke was born in 1883. When she was growing up, few women studied science. The ones who did usually became teachers. Clarke's goals were different. She wanted to become an electrical engineer. In 1919 she earned a degree in that field from the Massachusetts Institute of Technology (MIT). She was the first woman to earn this degree from MIT.

Edith Clarke, *right*, meets with a fellow engineer in a General Electric laboratory.

She then worked for General Electric for more than 25 years.

Each of these steps was rare for a woman of her time. But they were not all Clarke accomplished. She also received a patent for a device called the graphical calculator. This device helped solve math problems having to do with power systems. Her work helped the electric industry grow its networks of power lines. It also reduced the likelihood of power outages. When Clarke retired, she still was not done contributing to the field. She began teaching electrical engineering at the University of Texas in 1947. She was the first woman to teach this subject in the United States. Her work helped pave the way for other women.

Elsie Eaves

Elsie Eaves graduated from the University of Colorado in 1920. She earned a degree in civil engineering. After working for the government, Clark took a job with the *Engineering News-Record*. This business magazine provides news and opinions about the construction industry.

Today when people need to examine large amounts of data, they use computers. In the pre-computer era, Eaves created the first database of planned construction projects. After the end of World War II (1939–1945), a huge amount of construction took place in the United States. Eaves's database became a valuable resource. Both the government and private companies used it. It helped them decide which projects could be started and when.

Alva Matthews

Alva Matthews studied science at Middlebury and Barnard Colleges in the 1950s. She then earned her PhD in engineering science from Columbia University. It was becoming more common for women to study engineering during this time. But the change

Not Just a Pretty Face

Hedy Lamarr did not work as an engineer for a living. She was more famous for her career as an actress in the 1930s and 1940s. But in 1942, Lamarr helped invent a wireless communications system for torpedoes. The system switched radio frequencies rapidly. This prevented the enemy from blocking the signal. Decades later, a similar method was used to create modern wireless technologies.

Making Life Easier

Lillian Moller Gilbreth earned her PhD in 1915, a time when many women spent their days as homemakers. Gilbreth herself was a wife and mother of 12 children. She recognized the need for good tools for housework. Gilbreth began working for General Electric. She improved many kitchen appliances. She designed new ways to perform household tasks.

Gilbreth was also an expert in psychology. She found ways to make employees more satisfied. She went on to become the first female engineering professor at Purdue University. In 1966 Gilbreth became the first woman elected to the National Academy of Engineering.

was slow. Still, Matthews stood out for her work.

Her studies focused on shock waves. When a bomb goes off, the explosion causes sharp changes in pressure in all directions. The changes can affect air, soil, and even water. Matthews studied these changes using math. Her discoveries earned her a Society of Women Engineers award in 1971. Fellow engineers used her data to design safer ways to store military weapons.

Barbara Liskov is a computer science engineer. She is also a professor at MIT. Liskov didn't always have a clear career plan. She thinks that being flexible helped her succeed:

> I was never told that certain things shouldn't be done by women. I think this "ok" enabled me to follow my interest in math and science rather than settling on a more conventional direction. I find a career in engineering to be very satisfying. I like making things work. I also like finding solutions to problems that are both practical and elegant. And, I like working with a team of people; engineering involves lots of teamwork. I particularly like working with my students on our research projects. My advice to young women who are thinking about a career in engineering is to find out what is interesting to you and what you are good at. And be prepared to change your goals if that turns out to be the right thing for you.

> Source: "Barbara Liskov." Engineer Girl. National Academy of Engineering, 2016. Web. Accessed January 14, 2016.

Back It Up

Take a close look at this text. What parts of being an engineer does Liskov enjoy? What does Liskov think will help other women succeed in engineering? Back up your answers with evidence from the text.

CHAPTER THREE

MAKING A DIFFERENCE

Today's engineers have the benefit of using advanced technology in their work. Powerful computers let them design and collaborate more easily than ever before. Engineers are using these advantages to build an amazing future.

Nadine Harik

Nadine Harik has been an engineer at Pinterest since 2012. This popular website allows users to find and

Computers are important tools for modern engineers.

share photos. Harik oversees the company's web and mobile teams. Mobile users make up a large part of the website's traffic. Approximately 80 percent of the people who visit Pinterest do so from a mobile device.

Harik came to Pinterest after working as a senior software engineer at another web company, Google. She worked on some of Google's most important products, including YouTube. This work gave Harik valuable experience.

Merline Saintil

Merline Saintil oversees teams of engineers at Intuit. This software company creates computer programs for

More kids than ever before are learning to code. They may become the software engineers of tomorrow.

money management. One of its best-known products is the tax software TurboTax. Saintil is in charge of making these programs the best they can be. The website *Business Insider* listed her as one of 2014's most powerful female engineers. Before joining Intuit, Saintil worked at other leading technology companies, such as Adobe, PayPal, and Yahoo.

She thinks it is important for girls to learn about math, science, and engineering. In 2013 Saintil worked with US Representative Anna Eshoo of

23

California on the Congressional App Challenge. This contest asked kids to create apps and submit them to their representatives in Congress.

Saintil also thinks it is important for female engineers to support one another. She knows that being the only woman can be hard. She has been the only woman in classrooms and in offices. She conducts workshops so women can meet others who share their passion for engineering.

Kelly Bernish

Kelly Bernish is an environmental engineer. She is also the safety director for the city of Fort Collins, Colorado. In 2015 the American Society of Safety Engineers named Bernish its Safety Professional of the Year. In the past, Bernish was in charge of safety at Walt Disney World.

When Bernish began working in this field, many people did not understand what safety engineers did. Some didn't even think safety engineering was needed. But without these engineers, no one would make sure bridges and other structures were safe. Bernish worked hard to show people why it was important. She is proud of the difference she has made in her community.

Her advice for girls interested in engineering is to put their education first. She also recommends volunteering or working as an intern. That experience can be helpful down the road. She adds that finding a mentor is also important. So is connecting with peers who have similar interests.

Sounds of Engineering

Not all engineers build solid objects such as bridges or computers. Some create sound. Sylvia Massy is a sound engineer who produces popular music. She has worked with some big names in music, including the Red Hot Chili Peppers and Prince. She has worked on dozens of records. Massy is an excellent example of how creative engineers can be. Like other engineers, she gets to solve problems. Many times her work consists of letting the musicians play and figuring out what's missing. She then helps them add that to their songs.

CHAPTER FOUR

MOVING UP AND ADVANCING TECHNOLOGY

Engineering can be a path to many different careers. It can even lead women up the ladder to the highest positions in a company. Some women who move upward within a business keep doing engineering work. Others manage groups of engineers. These high-level engineers guide their employees in the right direction.

Marissa Mayer became CEO of the Internet company Yahoo! in 2012.

Unfair Treatment

Some men have become excellent mentors to female colleagues. But others do not treat female engineers respectfully. They may act unfriendly or hostile. Some even keep women from advancing. Many women refuse to give up because of this unfair, illegal treatment. But others end up leaving a company because of it. A few leave engineering altogether.

The treatment of women in the workplace has improved in recent decades. Legislators have created laws against workplace discrimination. Many female engineers join groups where they can meet with peers. They share experiences and discuss how to overcome challenges.

Ella Jobson

Ella Jobson is a senior design engineer at Caterpillar. This company builds construction equipment. She started out as a mechanical design engineer. At this time, Jobson was still working on her master's degree in engineering. Caterpillar gave her work that matched up with her course work. This let her put her education to use immediately. It also strengthened what she was learning.

Jobson later moved into structural design. In

Engineers design Caterpillar construction equipment that is used all around the world.

this role, she develops backhoe-loader machines and works on other projects. She also serves as a mentor to new engineers.

Lisa Su

Lisa Su is an electrical engineer. She has moved up the ranks in some of the top technology companies. She spent 13 years working for IBM. This company has played key roles in the history of computers. Su then moved on to AMD, a company that makes computer processors.

She became the company's senior vice president and general manager in 2012. Within only two more years, she became the company's chief executive officer (CEO). This is the highest position in a company. She no longer designs computer parts herself. She helps give AMD its overall direction. As she

Su poses with the material used to create advanced computer chips during her time at IBM.

Kullman speaks in a 2015 interview.

continues to lead AMD, Su hopes to push the industry forward.

Ellen Kullman

Ellen Kullman is a mechanical engineer. She worked as the CEO of DuPont. This chemical company has been around for more than 200 years. Running it earned Kullman a spot on *Forbes* magazine's 2015 list of the world's most powerful women.

Kullman earned her bachelor's degree from Tufts University. She later went back to school. She added a master's degree from Northwestern University. This degree was in management. She joined DuPont in 1988. Over time Kullman rose to the top spot in the company.

EXPLORE ONLINE

The focus of Chapter Four is successful female engineers. The below article from *Engineering and Technology Magazine* discusses whether engineering careers await women who want them. Each writer offers a different view. How does their information differ from what you have read in this chapter? What new information can you learn from this article?

Women in Engineering

mycorelibrary.com/women-in-engineering

CHAPTER FIVE

ENGINEERING THE FUTURE

Women have accomplished amazing feats in engineering. The past is filled with inspiring stories of female engineers. These innovators became role models for today's best and brightest engineers. But what does the future hold for women in the field?

At engineering camps and retreats, today's students are building amazing things, including hovercraft.

Do-It-Yourself Dollhouses

Many boys become interested in engineering after playing with building toys, such as construction sets. Girls can play with these toys too. But some girls prefer dollhouses and other traditional playthings. A California company wants to introduce those girls to building as well. Alice Brooks and Bettina Chen started Maykah, Inc. The company makes dollhouses. Kids can design the houses' lighting, elevators, and more. Brooks and Chen hope their toys inspire young girls to learn more about engineering.

Introducing Girls to Engineering

Engineers Week is held every February. This event has been around since 1951. It celebrates the difference engineers make in the world. It gets people talking about engineering and the need for more engineers. Kids, parents, and teachers are encouraged to participate.

One day during Engineers Week is Introduce a Girl to Engineering Day. Companies and schools invite young girls to visit and learn about

Building and testing bridges is one popular activity for students interested in engineering.

engineering. Students take part in hands-on activities. They learn about the work engineers do. Girls can also meet college engineering students, professors, and real-life engineers.

An Educational Getaway

In 2014 the University of California, Berkeley, held its first annual Girls in Engineering summer camp. Sixty middle-school girls visited the college. They learned about nanotechnology, optics, robotics, and other engineering subjects. The free weeklong event even included a field trip to Pixar Animation Studios. Pixar is the company that created films such as *Inside Out* and *Toy Story*.

Berkeley's faculty started the camp to let girls explore engineering careers through hands-on projects. Claire Tomlin is an engineering professor at the school. She sees the program as a way to show young girls that engineering can be fun.

Many other camps and programs have been set up throughout the country. Research has shown that by high school many girls become less open to studying math and science. These programs spark girls' interest and build their confidence before that happens.

Making Names for Themselves

The Institution of Engineering and Technology (IET) recognizes the top female innovators in engineering each year. The IET presents an annual prize called the

Young Woman Engineer of the Year award. The 2015 winner was Orla Murphy. She is an audio engineer at Jaguar Land Rover. Murphy combines her love of music with engineering. She improves the sound systems in her company's cars.

The Mary George Memorial Prize for Apprentices is given to a promising young engineer. The award goes to someone who others believe will soon become a leader in her field. Jessica Bestwick took home the prize in 2014. Bestwick works as a development engineer for automaker Rolls-Royce.

Engineering is all around us. From buildings

Making Connections

Being one of only a few women in a company can be hard. It can be helpful to talk to other women who do the same kind of work. The Society of Women Engineers (SWE) brings female engineers together. It also sponsors scholarships. SWE is a powerful voice for women in engineering. It is made up of approximately 30,000 women. The organization helps give female engineers a larger voice in this largely male field.

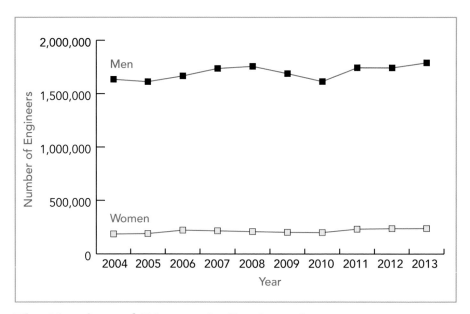

The Number of Women in Engineering
The overall number of women working as engineers is low compared with the number of men. But the numbers have increased somewhat in recent years. This graphs shows how many men and women were working as engineers in the United States in each year from 2004 to 2013. What do you think these numbers might look like ten years from now?

and bridges to cars and computers, the objects we use every day are designed by talented engineers. Imagine what the next generation of engineers will create. If you are interested in engineering, you may help build the world's future.

Erin Whitney attends high school in Maine. In 2015 her school's robotics team made it all the way to a major robotics championship. They placed thirteenth among their division of 75 teams. Whitney is the team's project manager. She offers the following advice to girls interested in engineering:

> My advice to young girls would be to never give up on your dreams, and don't ever let anyone tell you that you can't do something because you're a girl. Speaking from experience, people will question your intentions and try to deter you, but don't give up on your dreams just because someone tells you it's not right for girls to like math or science. There are so many historical women who were and are incredibly smart, and accomplished amazing things like helping create computers and landing the first man on the moon. You can be just like them. Your gender doesn't define how smart you are and you can do anything you set your mind to!
>
> Source: Erin Whitney. Personal Interview. October 27, 2015.

What's the Big Idea?
Take a close look at Whitney's advice for other girls interested in engineering and robotics. What is the main point she is making? What evidence does she use to support that point?

Join a Team

Does your school have a robotics team? These clubs learn about engineering so members can build robots. Many clubs participate in regional and national contests. If your school doesn't already have such a group, talk to one of your math or science teachers about starting one.

Buy a Kit

If you enjoy building things, you have already started down the road of engineering. Some companies sell kits that allow users to build customized robots and other high-tech objects. These advanced toys are a great way to learn about engineering.

Do You Have a Great Idea?

Many engineering marvels began with only a simple idea. Perhaps you have an idea for an invention. If so, start brainstorming ways you might be able to create this object. If you can't build it yet, what do you need to learn before you can?

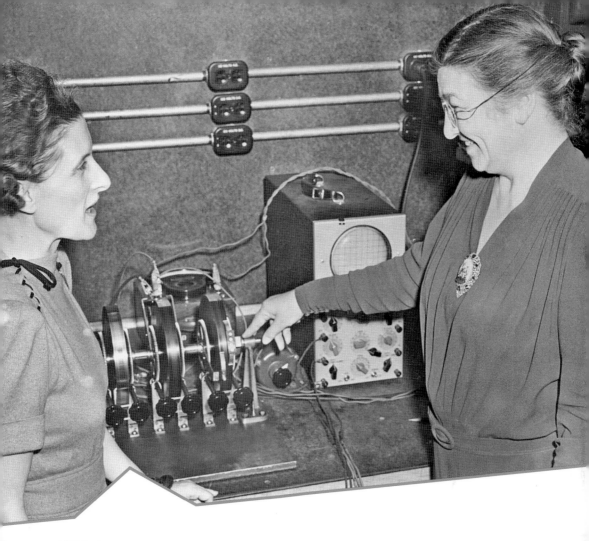

Job Shadow

Engineers work in many places. Make a list of the companies near you that employ different kinds of engineers. After deciding which type of engineering interests you most, contact a company to ask if you can spend a day observing a person who performs this kind of work.

Say What?

Learning about engineering can mean learning a lot of new vocabulary. Find five words in this book that you had never seen or heard before. Use a dictionary to find out what they mean. Write down the meaning of each word. Then use each word in a new sentence.

Why Do I Care?

Many female engineers have paved the way for other women to enter engineering fields. Why is it important for female engineers to mentor young women interested in engineering? Make a list of the ways that having an advisor would be helpful to you.

Tell the Tale

Pretend that you are getting ready for your first interview for an engineering job. Make a list of three questions that the interviewer might ask you. Then write a short response to each of them.

Surprise Me

Chapter Four shared information about female engineers at some big companies. After reading this book, what two or three facts about engineering jobs did you find most surprising? Write a few sentences about each fact. Why did you find each fact surprising?

GLOSSARY

audio
having to do with sound

discrimination
unfair treatment

infrastructure
the system of public works of a country, state, or region

mentor
a person who guides and advises a newer employee or younger person

patent
the exclusive right to profit from a product or design

processor
a tiny collection of electric circuits that is designed to carry out instructions

prototype
the first version of something that is built; it is used for testing

software
the programs and related information used by a computer

torpedo
a self-propelled submarine weapon

LEARN MORE

Books

May, Vicki V. *3-D Engineering.* White River
    Junction, VT: Nomad Press, 2015.

Miller, Reagan. *Engineering in Our Everyday Lives.*
    New York: Crabtree, 2014.

Websites

To learn more about Women in STEM, visit
booklinks.abdopublishing.com. These links are
routinely monitored and updated to provide the most
current information available.

Visit **mycorelibrary.com** for free additional tools for
teachers and students.

INDEX

Bernish, Kelly, 24–25

cars, 6, 7, 39–40
Clarke, Edith, 14–16
college, 6, 7, 30, 37
computers, 7, 9, 16, 19,
  21, 25, 30, 40–41
creativity, 6, 11, 25

da Vinci, Leonardo, 13

Eaves, Elsie, 16–17
engineering camps,
  37–38
engineering design
  process, 7

Gilbreth, Lillian Moller,
  18

Harik, Nadine, 21–22

Jobson, Ella, 28–29

kinds of engineers, 8
Kullman, Ellen, 32–33

Lamarr, Hedy, 17
Liskov, Barbara, 19

Massachusetts Institute
  of Technology (MIT),
  14, 19
Massy, Sylvia, 25
Matthews, Alva, 17–18

programming, 22–24

Saintil, Merline, 22–24
salaries, 10
Su, Lisa, 30–32

Women in Engineering,
  10
World War II, 17

ABOUT THE AUTHOR

Tammy Gagne has written more than 100 books for both adults and children. She resides in northern New England with her husband and son. One of her favorite pastimes is visiting schools to talk to children about the writing process.